PRAYING 101

for

MEN

By

Dottie Randazzo

Praying 101
for
Men

by

Dottie Randazzo

Creative Dreaming
6433 Topanga Cyn. Blvd.
120
Woodland Hills, CA 91303

ISBN 978-0-6151-5431-2

Never make the blunder of trying to forecast the way God is going to answer your prayer.

Oswald Chambers

By Dottie Randazzo

Praying 101 for Spiritual Enlightenment

Praying 101 for Kids & Teens

Praying 101 for Men

Praying 101 for Women

Praying 101 for Parents

Introduction

I realized a long time ago that most of us think that our prayers are not heard because we aren't getting what we want. But it's not that our prayers aren't heard; it's all in the asking. A few years ago, when a friend told me that he wanted something. I asked him if he'd said a prayer for it. He told me he didn't know how to pray.

As a child I attended both Baptist and Lutheran schools where I was taught how to memorize a few really good prayers, such as the Lord's Prayer. I was never really taught how to pray.

I know how to pray. I am not sure how I learned, but I did. All you have to do is ask my sister and she will tell you. She has often said I have a direct line to the heavens!

This book will teach you how to pray. It is your basic prayer book. I have designed a prayer for many aspects of your life. Once you have learned the key ingredients to praying you will have the tools to customize your own prayers. So let's flip the page and begin to solve the mystery of prayer.

Commonly Asked Questions

Do I need to know any special language to pray?

You do not need to know any special language. Your language and words will be understood.

Who do I pray to?

It does not matter whether you are praying to God. Our Father, The Masters of the Universe, or whomever, your prayer will be heard. Pray to the One that you believe in.

When and where should I pray?

Praying can be done anytime and anywhere. If you want to say your prayer in the morning, then that is when you should say it. If you want to say your prayer while driving to work, then that's when you should.

Do I have to kneel down or say my prayer out loud?

No kneeling needed. You can stand, lie down or be sitting in a park. It doesn't matter; your prayer will be heard. Your prayer does not need to be said out loud.

How do I pray?

To pray you use the little voice in your head. The same one that you hear when someone walks into the room with a weird hairdo and you hear in your head, *what was he thinking with that hair?* That's the same voice that you are going to say your prayer with. Those same voices in your head that you hear say, *I did well* or *I should not have done that.* It is almost like talking to yourself except you do it in your head. Say your prayer just like you are writing a letter; begin with "Dear_____." And always end your prayer with thanks. Thanks for listening, thanks for caring, thanks for looking out for me. Gratitude goes a long way in life.

If I don't get what I am asking for, does that mean my prayer was not heard?

Not getting what you want absolutely does not mean that your prayer was not heard. We always get what we want. We may not get it when we want it. We get it when we are supposed to.

Very Important Things You Should Know

Everything happens for a reason. . If something bad happens to you, you need to look at the experience and see what you were supposed to learn from it. For example, let's say you didn't get picked to play on the hockey league that you wanted. You are disappointed. You later learn that the night the hockey league plays is on the same night that you have a standing commitment. It's like someone was looking down on you and whispered to the hockey-picking-guy, "Don't pick him, he has to work late on Wednesdays." Remember the Universe is always looking out for you.

Everything happens exactly when it is supposed to. This might not be when you want it to happen. For example, let's say you keep applying for a promotion at work and each time you do not get it. You feel very discouraged. Years later you get the promotion. This promotion means you will be traveling a lot. If you take the time to look back you would see that the promotion would not have worked in your life before. You may have had small children or a sick elderly person to care for. Traveling with your job, at that time in your life, would not have worked. We get what we want when it is best for us.

You are doing in your life exactly what you are supposed to be doing at this exact moment. Every single moment in your life is very important and every single moment in your life affects the next moment in your life. Every person that you meet has a reason to be in your life, even if just for a brief moment. Some people come into our lives for a reason and some for a season.

Enjoy your life. You must learn to enjoy your life. Eating your breakfast in the morning is part of your life. Don't sit down and eat it fast while you are thinking of something else. This is a very bad habit to start. It will take you twice as long to fix the bad habit. Every single day is a very important day in your life. It is a day that you will never get to relive. Learn to appreciate every moment and don't take them for granted.

Pray for wisdom. Wisdom is smarts, answers, solutions and brainpower. When you ask for wisdom you ask to be aware of the right answers. Wisdom allows you to see answers when they enter your life. For example, when I first started my legal service I felt alone. I didn't know anyone else who was starting a business. I prayed that the loneliness be removed. I thought I would just wake up one day and not feel lonely anymore. Instead, I attended a training seminar and began talking to the woman next to me who had also just started a business. We became friends and shared a lot of new business information. The lonely feeling was gone. I never imagined that my prayer would be answered that way, but it was. Sometimes we get answers but they don't always come to us the way we think that they should and therefore we don't see the answer. We miss them because we are looking for them to be delivered our way. Answers are delivered the way that they are supposed to be delivered, not necessarily the way that we want them delivered.

Believe that your prayers are heard and will be answered. Why pray if you don't have any faith. The bible says that faith the size of a mustard seed can move a mountain. Like Wow! Have you ever seen a mustard seed? It's tiny. Don't try praying to test the system. It doesn't work. The system does not need to be tested by you.

Prayer for Good Health

Dear Lord,

I pray for the wisdom to maintain/obtain a good strong healthy body. I pray for the awareness that my body is a reflection of your creation and it is perfect in every way. Thank you for taking care of me.

Prayer to Move Beyond an Abusive Relationship

Dear God,

I pray for the strength, courage and wisdom to move beyond the abusive relationship I am in. I pray for the courage to stand up for my beliefs and myself. I pray for the strength not to be bullied into a bad situation just to be accepted. I pray for the wisdom to be able to see the lesson in this situation and to grow from it in a positive way. Thank you for blessing me.

Prayer to Resolve Impotence

Dear Masters of the Universe,

I pray for the wisdom to make the correct choices regarding my health. I pray that I will be guided towards the best treatment for me. I pray that you remove any feelings of insecurity that I possess. Thank you for taking care of me.

Prayer for Good Health for Someone Else

Dear Goddess,

I pray and ask you to bless my friend/relative with good health. I pray that they will have the wisdom to see and make the correct choices for their health. I pray that you remove any feelings of insecurity that they may possess. Thank you for listening to me.

Prayer for Better Relationships

(With Parents, Siblings, Spouses and/or Children)

Dear Higher Power,

I pray for the wisdom to develop positive relationships with those that I love. I pray for the wisdom to understand them. I pray that they have the wisdom to understand me. Thank you for listening to me.

Prayer for Safety in Travels or Vacations

Dear Father,

I pray for the wisdom to make the correct choices regarding my safety and the safety of others while traveling and/or on vacation. Thank you for taking care of me.

Prayer to Remove Loneliness

Dear Lord,

I pray for the wisdom and strength to remove the loneliness that I feel inside. I pray that you will send someone into my life to have fun and share my life with. I pray that you remove any feelings of insecurity that I possess. I pray for the wisdom to be able to see the lesson in this situation and to grow from it in a positive way. I pray for the wisdom to love my body. I pray for the awareness that my body is a reflection of your creation and it is perfect in every way. Thank you for blessing me.

Prayer to Listen to My Intuition

Dear God,

I pray for the wisdom to learn how to listen to my intuition. I pray for the wisdom to be able to see the correct choices in life. Thank you for listening to me.

Prayer Because I am too Thin or Anorexic

Dear Masters of the Universe,

I pray for the wisdom to be able to identify bad eating habits from healthy ones. I pray that others will not judge me because of my weight and that they will see me for the great person that I am in on the inside. I pray for the wisdom to be able to see the lesson(s) in this situation and to grow from it in a positive way. I pray for the wisdom to love my body. I pray for the awareness that my body is a reflection of your creation and it is perfect in every way. I pray for good health. I pray that you remove any feelings of insecurity that I possess. Thank you for taking care of me.

Prayer to Overcome Insomnia

Dear Goddess,

I pray that you will free my mind of all worry. I pray for the wisdom to release all tension in my body. I pray for the strength and courage to know that my life is exactly as it should be at every given moment. I pray for relaxation and a peaceful night of sleep. Thank you for listening to me.

Prayer for Better Finances

Dear Higher Power,

I pray for the wisdom to understand my finances. I pray for the strength and the courage not to waste money. I pray for the wisdom to see the correct choices for my finances. Thank you for blessing me.

Prayer to Overcome Hate and Anxiety

Dear Father,

I pray for the wisdom, courage and strength to remove the hate that I feel for another individual. I pray for the wisdom to remove all anxiety that I am suffering from. I pray for the wisdom to replace those feelings of hate and anxiety with feelings of compassion and understanding. I pray for the courage to stand up for my beliefs and myself. I pray for the strength not to be bullied into a bad situation just to fit in. I pray for the wisdom to be able to see the lesson in this situation and to grow from it in a positive way. I pray that you remove any feelings of insecurity that I possess. Thank you for taking care of me.

Prayer to Cope with Balding

Dear Lord,

I pray for the strength and courage to overcome any humiliation that I may feel by losing my hair. I pray that others will not judge me because I am balding and that they will see me for the great person that I am on the inside. I pray for the wisdom to be able to see the lesson in this situation and to grow from it in a positive way. I pray for the wisdom to love my body. I pray for the awareness that my body is a reflection of your creation and it is perfect in every way. I pray that you remove any feelings of insecurity that I possess. Thank you for blessing me.

Prayer for Wisdom to See and Make the Correct Choice

Dear God,

I pray for the wisdom to see and make the correct choices in all areas of my life. I pray for the wisdom to be able to see the lessons necessary for me to learn and to grow from them in a positive way. I pray that you remove any feelings of insecurity that I possess. Thank you for taking care of me.

Prayer for Better Memory

Dear Masters of the Universe,

I pray for the wisdom to have better memory. I pray that you remove any feelings of insecurity that I possess. Thank you for listening to me.

Prayer to Overcome Addictions
(Gambling, Anorexia, Bulimia, Drugs, Alcohol, Smoking)

Dear Goddess,

I pray for the wisdom, strength and courage to recognize things in my life that will help me overcome my addiction(s). I pray for the wisdom to make the correct choices and to stand up for my beliefs and myself and not to be bullied into a bad situation just to fit in. I pray for the wisdom to love my body. I pray for the awareness that my body is a reflection of your creation and it is perfect in every way. I pray that you remove any feelings of insecurity that I possess. Thank you for listening to me.

Prayer to Tell the Truth and Not Lie

Dear Higher Power,

I pray for the wisdom, strength and courage to tell the truth and not lie. I pray that I will have the courage to stand up for my beliefs and myself and not to be bullied into a bad situation just to fit in. Thank you for blessing me.

Prayer for Divorced Parents

Dear Father,

I pray that you will bless both of my parents and guide them with the wisdom to see and make the correct choices regarding our family. I pray that you will remove any hurt, hate or unhealthy feelings from my family. I pray that you will bless us with an abundance of understanding. I pray for the wisdom to be able to see the lesson in this situation and to grow from it in a positive way. I pray that you remove any feelings of insecurity that I possess. Thank you for taking care of me.

Prayer for Dealing with the Death of a Loved One

Dear Lord,

I pray that my loved one is safe, sound, taken care of, happy and free of any pain or illness. I pray for the strength and courage to go on with my life. I pray for the wisdom to understand this loss. I pray for the wisdom and strength not to let my emotions disable my life. I pray that you remove any pain or loneliness that I feel in my heart. Thank you for taking care of me.

Prayer for Sports

Dear God,

I pray for the wisdom to perfect my skills and talents regarding my favorite sports. I pray for the wisdom to be aware of the opportunities to become better at my favorite sport. I pray for my safety and the safety of others while I am participating in my favorite sports. I pray that you remove any feelings of insecurity that I possess. Thank you for blessing me.

Prayer for New Home and Neighborhood

Dear Masters of the Universe,

I pray that you will bless our new home and neighborhood. I pray for the safety of my family in our new home and neighborhood. I pray that you will bless us with an abundance of happy memories in our new home and neighborhood. I pray that you remove any feelings of insecurity that I possess. Thank you for taking care of me.

Prayer for Love

Dear Goddess,

I pray to be blessed with unconditional love. I pray for the wisdom to love others unconditionally. Thank you for looking out for me.

Prayer to Overcome Panic Attacks

Dear Higher Power,

I pray for the wisdom, strength and courage to overcome my panic attacks. I pray for the wisdom to be able to see the lesson in this situation and to grow from it in a positive way. I pray for the wisdom to love my body. I pray for the awareness that my body is a reflection of your creation and it is perfect in every way. I pray that you remove any feelings of insecurity that I possess. Thank you for blessing me.

Prayer for
Self-Esteem and Self-Worth

Dear Father,

I pray that you bless me with an abundance of self-esteem and self-worth. I pray for the wisdom to be able to distinguish self-destructive behavior from productive healthy behavior. I pray that I never forget my self-worth. I pray for the strength and courage to stand up for my beliefs and myself and not to be bullied into a bad situation just to fit in. I pray for the wisdom to love my body. I pray for the awareness that my body is a reflection of your creation and it is perfect in every way. Thank you for listening to me.

Prayer for Creativity

Dear Lord,

I pray for creativity on my project. I pray for the wisdom to recognize the creative signs that are being shown to me. I pray for enthusiasm and motivation. I pray for the strength to overcome procrastination. Thank you for taking care of me.

Prayer for Pregnancy

Dear God,

I pray for the wisdom to make correct choice. I pray for the health of my family. I pray for the strength and courage to stand up for my beliefs and not to be bullied into a bad situation just to fit in. I pray for the wisdom to be able to see the lesson in this situation and to grow from it in a positive way. Thank you for listening to me.

Prayer to Overcome Unemployment

Dear Masters of the Universe,

I pray for the wisdom to find employment. I pray for the wisdom to see the correct choices for me. I pray for the wisdom to learn what skills, training and/or education I need to make me more employable. I pray for you to remove any insecurity that I may possess. I pray for the wisdom to see the lesson in this situation and to grow from it in a positive way. I pray for the wisdom to remove any anxiety or confusion. I pray for confidence in my abilities. I pray for enthusiasm and motivation. I pray for the strength to overcome procrastination. Thank you for blessing me.

Prayer for Unlimited Personal Power

Dear Goddess,

Thank you for providing me with unlimited personal power on a daily basis. Thank you for the wisdom to realize that happiness and fulfillment come from inside me.

Prayer for Good Judgment

Dear Higher Power,

I pray for the wisdom to identify correct choices
and to exercise good judgment in every area of
my life. Thank you for blessing me.

Prayer for My Sexuality

Dear Father,

I pray for the wisdom to identify and make correct choices regarding my sexuality. I pray for the strength and courage to stand up for my beliefs and myself and not to be bullied into a bad situation just to fit in. I pray that others will see me for the person that I am on the inside and not judge me by my sexual preferences. I pray for the wisdom to love my body. I pray that you will protect me from evil. I pray for the awareness that my body is a reflection of your creation and it is perfect in every way. I pray that you remove any feelings of insecurity that I possess. Thank you for looking out for me.

Prayer for Hobbies

Dear Lord,

I pray for the wisdom to perfect my skills and talents regarding my hobby or hobbies. I pray for the wisdom to be aware of the opportunities to become better at my hobby or hobbies. I pray for my safety and the safety of others while I am participating in my hobby or hobbies. I pray that you remove any feelings of insecurity that I possess. Thank you for listening to me.

Prayer for Mental Strength and Courage

Dear God,

I pray for mental strength and courage. I pray for the wisdom to make the correct choices and to stand up for my beliefs and myself. I pray for the courage not to be bullied into a bad situation just to fit in. I pray that you remove any feelings of insecurity that I possess. Thank you for looking out for me.

Prayer to Be True to Yourself

Dear Masters of the Universe,

I pray for the courage to stand up for my beliefs and myself. I pray for the courage not to be bullied into a bad situation just to fit in. I pray for the wisdom to love my body. Thank you for taking care of me.

Prayer for Adoption

Dear Goddess,

I pray for the wisdom to make the correct choices regarding adoption. I pray that you remove any insecurity I possess. Thank you for blessing me.

Prayer to Learn Life's Purpose

Dear Higher Power,

I pray for the wisdom to learn what my life's purpose is. I pray that my intuition will guide me in the right direction. I pray that I will see the correct choices. I pray for the wisdom to remove any anxiety or confusion. I pray for confidence in my abilities. Thank you for taking care of me.

Prayer to Better My Career

Dear Father,

I pray for the wisdom to acquire a better job or get the promotion that I want. I pray for the wisdom to be able to see the lesson in this situation and to grow from it. If it isn't meant for me to have this position, I pray for the wisdom to understand why. Thank you for listening to me.

Prayer to Live in the Moment

Dear Lord,

I pray for the wisdom to be aware each and every day of my special life. I pray for the wisdom to not take anything for granted and to be gracious of the gift of life. Thank you for blessing me.

Prayer for Happiness

Dear God,

I pray that you will bless me and those around me with an abundance of happiness. Thank you for blessing me.

Prayer to Forgive Someone

Dear Masters of the Universe,

I pray for the wisdom, strength, courage and compassion to forgive the individual who I feel has betrayed me. I pray for the wisdom to see and make the correct choices in this situation. I pray for the courage to stand up for my beliefs and myself. I pray for the strength not to be bullied into a bad situation just to fit in. I pray for the wisdom to be able to see the lesson in this situation and to grow from it in a positive way. Thank you for taking care of me.

Prayer for Peace and Contentment without Worry, Stress or Anxiety

Dear Goddess,

I pray that you will bless me with peace and contentment. I pray for the wisdom to remove all worry from my soul. I pray for the strength and courage to recognize contentment without worry. I pray for the wisdom to remove all stress and anxiety. I pray that you remove any feelings of insecurity that I possess. Thank you for listening to me.

Prayer for New School or New Job

Dear Higher Power,

I pray that you will remove any fear or anxiety from me about attending my new school or new job. I pray that you will protect me from all harm and evil people. I pray for the wisdom to make new friends and see enemies. I pray for the courage to stand up for my beliefs and myself. I pray for the courage not to be bullied into a bad situation just to fit in. I pray for the wisdom to learn what is being taught to me. I pray that you remove any feelings of insecurity that I possess. Thank you for taking care of me.

Prayer to Get the Message

Dear Father,

I pray for the wisdom to learn what I am suppose to learn during my time here on earth. I pray that I will be guided and protected as I walk through life. I pray for the wisdom to see the daily miracles that are so graciously sprinkled in my life. Thank you for taking care of me.

Prayer for Aging with Dignity

Dear Lord,

I pray that you bless me with self-love. I pray for the wisdom to see and make the correct choices in my life. I pray for the wisdom to love my body. I pray for the awareness that my body is a reflection of your creation and it is perfect in every way. I pray that you remove any feelings of insecurity that I possess. Thank you for listening to me.

Prayer for Selflessness

Dear God,

I pray for the wisdom to be selfless. I pray that I will be able to help others when needed and not expect anything from them. I am constantly reminded that the payback for selflessness is a life sprinkled with miracles. I pray that I am able to care for others from the goodness of my heart. I pray that I have the strength and courage to stand up for my beliefs and courage to stand up for myself. I pray for the courage not to be bullied into a bad situation just to fit in. Thank you for listening to me.

Prayer to Overcome Confusion

Dear Masters of the Universe,

I am confused and do not know what decision is the correct decision. I pray for a sign that will show me the correct decision. I pray for the wisdom that I will recognize the sign when presented to me. I pray for the courage to stand up for my beliefs and myself. I pray for the courage not to be bullied into a bad situation just to fit in. I pray for the wisdom to be able to see the lesson in this situation and to grow from it in a positive way. Thank you for taking care of me.

Prayer for Marriage, Commitment, Relationship and/or Companionship

Dear Goddess,

I pray that you bless me with a wonderful mate. I pray for the wisdom to see and make the correct choices. I pray that you protect me from evil people. I pray for the strength and the courage to have the patience for the right person to come into my life. I pray that you remove any feelings of insecurity that I possess. Thank you for listening to me.

Prayer for Authentic Success

Dear Higher Power,

I pray for the wisdom to make the time to pursue the personal goals that bring me pleasure. I pray for the wisdom to make the time for my family, my garden, my home and my soul. I pray that if today was my last day on earth that I would leave with no regrets. I pray for the wisdom to feel focused. I pray for the wisdom to accept my limitations and make peace with past. I pray for the wisdom to discover and call forth my gifts and offer them to the world. Thank you for taking care of me.

Prayer to Recognize the Enemy Within

Dear Father,

I pray for the wisdom to realize that I am my own worst enemy. I pray for the wisdom to stop feeling sorry for myself. I pray for the courage to stop the fear before it stops my dreams from materializing. I pray for the wisdom to observe my behavior and make necessary positive changes. Thank you for loving me.

Prayer for Constant Craving

Dear Lord,

I pray for the wisdom to make contentment my constant craving. I pray for the wisdom to make moments of self-nurturance that bring contentment. I pray for the wisdom to see what I really need to be content. Thank you for listening to me.

Prayer for Feeling Great

Dear God,

I pray that you bless me with great feelings. I am eternally thankful for everything that I have been blessed with in my life. Thank you for listening to me.

Prayer for Recognizing Burnout

Dear Masters of the Universe,

I pray for the wisdom to recognize that burnout is caused by not having a balanced life. I pray for the wisdom, strength and courage to make the changes in my lifestyle that need to be made. Thank you for loving me.

Prayer to Recognize Buried Dreams

Dear Goddess,

I pray for the wisdom to remember that today is a day for being. I pray for the wisdom to remember to be with those that I love and to be kind to myself. I pray for the courage to be silent and call forth the dream that I buried so long ago. I pray for the wisdom to see it in my mind and hold it in my heart. Thank you for loving me.

Prayer for Blessing our Circumstances

Dear Higher Power,

I pray for the wisdom to realize that even though I don't know right now why this thing and/or event has occurred I do know, that once there is enough distance, I will be able to look back and see the reason. I pray that you bless this circumstance and that by surrendering it to you I am learning to trust. Thank you for taking care of me.

Prayer to Love a Good Partner

Dear Father,

Thank you for blessing me with this wonderful partner in my life. I pray for the wisdom and courage to give her all the love that she desires and deserves. Thank you for listening to me.

Prayer for Emotional Availability

Dear Lord,

I pray for the wisdom, strength and courage to be emotionally available for friends and family. I pray for the wisdom to understand that emotions such as sadness, hurt, pain, joy and love are healthy emotions. I pray that you remove any feelings of weakness that I may feel when the need arises for me to express them. Thank you for taking care of me.

Prayer to Overcome Getting Dumped

Dear God,

I pray for the wisdom, strength and courage to overcome the feelings of abandonment and rejection. I pray for the wisdom, strength and courage to see the lesson that I am suppose to learn from this experience. I pray that you remove the feelings of hurt, sadness and loneliness. I pray for the wisdom to understand that I am a good person. I pray for the strength to wait for that special person you are sending into my life. Thank you for listening to me.

Prayer for Eliminating the Need to Control

Dear Masters of the Universe,

I pray for the wisdom, strength and courage to be able to let go of the need to always be in control. I pray for the wisdom, strength and courage to relax and let my life unfold in front of me just as you planned. Thank you for loving me.

Prayer to be a People Magnet

Dear Goddess,

I pray for the wisdom to have charisma. I pray for the wisdom to attract wonderful people in my life. I pray for the strength and courage to be myself. Thank you for taking care of me.

Prayer to Remain Sober

Dear Higher Power,

I pray for the wisdom to remember that today is a day for being. I pray for the wisdom to remember to be with those that I love and to be kind to myself. I pray for the strength and courage to live one day at a time. I pray for the strength and courage to just say "no". Thank you for loving me.

Prayer to Overcome Egotism

Dear Father,

I pray for the wisdom, strength and courage to realize it isn't all about me. I pray for the wisdom to put myself in another's place. I pray for the wisdom to make unbiased decisions that are in the best interest of all parties involved. Thank you for blessing me.

Prayer for Getting Unstuck or Solving a Problem

Dear Lord,

I pray for the wisdom to become unstuck and solve my problem. I pray for the wisdom to be able to relax and remain quite so that I can see and hear the solution when it is sent to me. Thank you for listening to me.

Prayer to Release Pettiness

Dear God,

I pray for the wisdom, strength and courage to be able to release pettiness. I pray for the wisdom, strength and courage to not make a big deal out of the small stuff. Thank you for loving me.

Prayer for Starting Over

Dear Masters of the Universe,

I pray for the wisdom, strength and courage to begin my life anew. I pray that I will be guided in the right direction. I pray for the wisdom to be able to move forward with my life. I pray for the wisdom, strength and courage to be able to leave the past in the past. Thank you for blessing me.

Prayer to Overcome Depression

Dear Goddess,

I pray for the wisdom, strength and courage to remove my depressed state of mind. I pray for the wisdom to remember every morning that I have a choice regarding what I am going to think about and how I am going to feel during the day. I pray for the wisdom, strength and courage that I will be guided in ways that will help me overcome my depression. Thank you for blessing me.

Prayer for When a Friendship Hurts

Dear Higher Power,

I pray that you will heal my hurt feelings. I pray for the wisdom to learn from this hurtful incident. I pray for the wisdom, strength and courage not to harbor resentment or vindictive feelings. I pray that you will bless this person who has hurt me. I pray for peace and contentment. Thank you for loving me.

Prayer for Volunteer Work

Dear Father,

I pray for the wisdom to recognize the opportunity for volunteer work where I will best be able to serve and help others. I pray for the strength and courage to stand up for my beliefs. Thank you for listening to me.

Prayer to Remain Celibate

Dear Lord,

I pray for the strength and courage to be celibate. I pray that all temptation be eliminated from my life. I pray for the strength and courage to stand up for my beliefs and not to be bullied into a situation just to fit in. Thank you for blessing me.

Prayer to Overcome Embarrassment

Dear God,

I pray for the wisdom to overcome my embarrassment. I pray for the courage and strength to forgive the individuals who had or have any involvement with my embarrassment. I pray for the wisdom to see the lesson I am suppose to learn in this situation. I pray for the strength and courage to stand up for my beliefs and not to be bullied into a situation just to fit in. Thank you for taking care of me.

Prayer to Overcome Insensitivity

Dear Masters of the Universe,

I pray for the wisdom to remove my insensitivity. I pray for the wisdom to learn the lesson in this situation. I pray for compassion, sensitivity and understanding. Thank you for blessing me.

Prayer to Overcome Cheating

Dear Goddess,

I pray for forgiveness for my cheating. I pray that you remove the pain and suffering that I have caused in others. I pray for the wisdom to learn the lesson in this situation. I pray for the strength and courage to not cheat again. I pray for the strength and courage to stand up for my beliefs and not to be bullied into a situation just to fit in. Thank you for taking care of me.

Prayer for Being Fired from a Job

Dear Higher Power,

I pray for the wisdom to learn the lessons from this situation. I pray that I have the wisdom to see the new opportunities that are being presented to me. I pray that you remove any insecurity that I may possess. Thank you for blessing me.

Prayer for Sharing

Dear Father,

I pray for the wisdom to allow myself to share with others. I pray that I have the courage to share my time, my love, my attention, my knowledge and my material possessions. I pray for the wisdom to know that sharing these things is what makes them so valuable. Thank you for listening to me.

Prayer to Overcome Road Rage

Dear Lord,

I pray for the wisdom to learn to control my road rage. I pray for the safety and the safety of others. I pray that I have the wisdom to learn from this experience. Thank you for looking out for me.

Prayer to Release Forcefulness

Dear God,

I pray for the wisdom to learn why I feel the
need to be forceful with friends and family. I
pray for the wisdom to learn how this affects
my relationships with those around me. I pray
for the strength to be able to control myself
before letting my forcefulness affect a situation.
I pray for the wisdom to learn from this
situation. Thank you for listening to me.

Prayer for Goal Achievement

Dear Masters of the Universe,

I pray for the wisdom to achieve my goal. I pray that I will be able to see and identify every opportunity that is necessary for me to achieve my goal. If it is not in my best interest to achieve this goal, I pray for the wisdom to be able to identify why. Thank you for blessing me.

Prayer to Overcome Forgetfulness

Dear Goddess,

I pray for the wisdom to overcome my forgetfulness. I pray for the wisdom to be able to see and identify what I need to overcome my forgetfulness. I pray that I will be able to see the lesson necessary for me to learn regarding my forgetfulness. Thank you for looking out for me.

Prayer Not to Lose Control

Dear Higher Power,

I pray for the wisdom to be aware of the benefits of not losing control. I pray for the strength and courage to stay in control. I pray for the strength and courage not to be bullied into a bad situation just to fit in. Thank you for blessing me.

Prayer for Forgiveness

Dear Father,

I pray for the wisdom to be aware of the benefits of forgiveness. I pray for the strength and courage to be able to forgive myself and others. I pray that you remove any insecurity that I may possess. Thank you for loving me.

Prayer for Better Communications

Dear Lord,

I pray for the wisdom to be aware of the benefits of better communications. I pray for the wisdom to be aware of the many opportunities that are available to me for better communications. I pray that you remove any insecurity that I possess. Thank you for blessing me.

My Personalized Prayers

My Personalized Prayers

PRAYER FOR/TO

www.ingramcontent.com/pod-product-compliance
Lightning Source LLC
Chambersburg PA
CBHW032015040426
42448CB00006B/642